Some Sweet Vandal

Some Sweet Vandal

Poems By

James Dickson

Cover design by Shay Culligan
Cover art by Greer Proctor-Dickson
Author photo by Greer Proctor-Dickson

ISBN: 978-1-63980-118-3

Kelsay Books
502 South 1040 East, A-119
American Fork, Utah 84003
Kelsaybooks.com

*For Greer, who told me so,
and James, my favorite poem.*

In memory of Billy Avalon. Follow, poet.

Acknowledgments

Thanks are due to the following journals for giving these poems their first printings:

Amoskeag: "Honda Concerto"
The Bosphorus Art Project Quarterly: "Punch Lines"
Evening Street Review: "In Peace"
The Fiddleback: "Reckless," from "Each Empty Desk"
Glassworks: "Instructional"
Two Hawks Quarterly: "If Basho Taught High School"
Hospital Drive: "Punctuation"
The Louisiana Review: "The Old Lie"
Ruminate: "Lost in Translation"
Slant: "Circadian Arrhythmia"
Spillway: "Seasonal"
Stirrings: "Outage Cycle"
Sylvia: "After a Faculty Meeting, I Read Plath," from
     "Three for Sylvia"
The Tipton Poetry Journal: "Coastline"
Poetry Quarterly: "Exodus"

"In Peace" also appears in *A Ritual to Read Together: Poems in Conversation with William Stafford,* edited by Becca J.R. Lachman

"Mother's Day Plans" was selected as a finalist for *Ruminate's* McCabe Poetry Prize

The following people and institutions deserve more thanks than can be printed:

• Ed Ochester, Tim Liu, Major Jackson, April Bernard. Junie Levin, and V, who keeps us together

• Caitlin McKinzie, Becca Lachman, Elijah Burrell, Christian Anton Gerard, Willa Carrol, Liz Wittee. Also, Heather Dobbins and Adam Clay, for getting things in order.

• The English Department and administration of Germantown High School. Thanks for so much.

• The staff of *The Agathist*. The Civic is a lie.

• The Mississippi Arts Commission, whose financial generosity made several of these poems possible.

• My parents, Andy and Beejee, for the poet's burden of a loving, supportive family.

Contents

Kokopelli

Some sweet vandal has coronated
the handrail with a chain

of woven clover blossoms.
I was surprised to see

my students leave the helix
intact. Avoiding the rail,

they leaned under their backpacks,
teetering against beauty's uselessness.

Lift

The cut cedar bleeds its odor,
sharp, like
copper on the tongue.

Another branch on the fire,
snaps like laughter
of children at play.

Sparks spiral skyward,
star-bound and mixing with the stars,
infinite pinpoints.

A prayer for a suffering friend rises too.
Whitman says "all goes onward
And outward, nothing collapses."

The cedar branches dissolve
Into themselves; she said
My life is caving in

but the embers tumble up,
releasing themselves into the hot night,
not gone.

Their stellar nebulas etch themselves
into my retinas, flashing every
time I close my eyes.

Punctuation

—for Lucy, who came back to school

The scar begins behind her ear
and slithers its way around to
her forehead, ending above her
right eyebrow, like a question mark.

What is it asking? Is the scar itself
a cosmic joke? A nasty coincidence?
How & why did she survive, outliving
the twisted ampersand of her car?

She wears other marks, each one
like functional jewelry: the colon
of her stoma between her clavicles.
The parenthetic wheelchair cradling

(not confining) her body,
bent like a comma.

Fear and Wonder

Angelic isn't the right word:
angels always scared the hell
out of people when they spoke.
This was different. Something

lucid, a completeness holy
men have sought for centuries
but never expected to find
in a bar, on open-mic night

as two girls harmonized
Be thou my vision,
O Lord of my heart
and everything—the drinks,

the flirting, even the bartender
crashing bottles into the trash—
stopped. The din fell silent
under their pure light of song.

Honda Concerto

Heard melodies are sweet, but those unheard are sweeter.
                                                —Keats

Windows rolled down in his crappy
old Honda, the heavy metal kid
holds concert. The car's tinny speakers
try to outscream him as tattooed
arms fly, pounding steering wheel
and invisible cymbals.

His audience continues crossing,
making their protected left turns,
glancing through their tightly
raised windows at the dangerous
wonder of his song.

If Basho Buried Students

I visit their graves, and Boncho's
poem to his dead teacher
drifts into my mind.

At dear Basho's grave
Pale thin transients, we pause—
spring mist, sad pupil.

I become Boncho's
negative: a sad teacher
bullied by dead leaves.

*

Blank pages litter
my desk and pencil shavings
scatter like ashes.

Each Empty Desk

I with no rights in this matter; neither father nor lover.
—Roethke

Prologue:

Eight students dead my first twelve years,
but the funerals haven't
whittled me down:
a knife's stroke
is too calculated, too clean.

Instead I am burred, hacked;
dusty refuse on the workroom floor.

Chapter 1: Reckless

(for Ryan)

I think about you racing,
the red light, the third-degree
burns over half your body,

about you in 9th grade, the only
student to answer "Tybalt"
when I asked who was to blame
for Romeo and Juliet's deaths.

He was reckless, you said.

Chapter 2: Pull

(for Blake)

Chris winced
in his desk, craned
his neck to the left,
knuckled the knot
in his shoulder.

He was a pallbearer yesterday.

Last year, I cornered Blake
with this cliché:
You're only hurting yourself
when you get too stoned
to show up to class.

Now, one run red-light later,
I watch Chris grimace,
and I realize how wrong I was.

In Peace

The Army recruiter
interrupts my class
and pitches this line:
Give us your best,
we'll give you the rest.

I imagine this rest my students
might get—flag-shrouded,
tidy rows, like kindergarten
cots at nap time.

Three for Sylvia

1.
Hartsdale Drive, 2004

I breathe back from a stack of students' poems.
Next up, Courtney's elegy for Sylvia Plath,
dense with imagery and intensity.

In 1953, Richard Wilbur saw himself
as I see me: a fool watching
such talent toil in fragility.

What do I say to this page, with its broken
razor blades swirling in an unstarred sky?
I'm scared that, like Wilbur, I will have to write

an elegy too soon, Court's pen replaced
by a fistful of pills. I am a stupid lifeguard,
watching her drown, she a brilliant negative,

blind to herself.

2.
Bite

What a thrill!
My thumbnail instead of a meal.
The red horseshoes behind,
threatening the pale half-moon.

It's a filthy, tragic love,
that happy dagger:
the nail between incisors
the satisfaction

of penetration: this ugly
cut, leaving a
jagged crescent on my
hand and its puzzle-piece

mate in my mouth.
A cold-turkey relapse:
junkies know nothing, perhaps,
of my shakes, my false starts

my lust for that sweet stab,
that tingle of wrong. To pluck
that apple off of my finger's
tree, to ravish the intruder

creeping beyond its numb
round boundary.
Dirty boy,
bitten thumb.

3.
After a Faculty Meeting, I Read Plath

I will die again. A school-shooter
simulation, and my boss tells me
the medics need a victim.

Dying is an art,
and mine is scheduled:
February 11.

*

After school, other teachers brought in
to play students. Shooter man, shooter man,

your Aryan eye peers over the muzzle-capped
rifle. I have always been scared of you, yet I stand,

run. *No, don't shoot.* But you do. Your blanks
crackle. Each dead child coils down. Over the

intercom, our lockdown code melts into a shriek
of sirens, shouts. Fake blood floods to a spot

on my shirt. Waiting for the paramedics to black-
tag me, I eat time like air.

Outage Cycle

I'm still flipping switches
exiting and entering rooms.
The power has been out for days,
but muscle memory is more powerful
than the winds that put us in the dark.

The squirrels suffer from this amnesia, too:
they scamper across the ground and up
the truncated pines, whose top halves now
lie cut and stacked on the front curb,
radiating a harrowing pine odor,

as Neruda wrote, that mingles
with the singe of grills charring
meat from now-warm freezers to create
the incense that rises over all neighborhoods
as they emerge from a storm's wreckage.

Also part of this liturgy—the choir
of soprano chainsaws harmonizing with
the emphysema rattle of diesel-engined trucks
with strobing jaundice lights
that fill rooms like the one I'm in now,

as I sit and write these words under
the lamp that will not come on, regardless
of how many times the chain gets pulled.

The Old Lie

—for Billy
il miglior insegnante

I was impressed with myself, commanding
these 10th graders' attention this Friday
afternoon in my windowless cinder-pod.
The storm outside followed my reading
of "Charge of the Light Brigade"
like a soundtrack, thundering to left and
right, fading as the noble ones fell.

Next, the contrast piece—"Dulce et Decorum Est,"
and I might as well be orchestrating
their breathing. We're there, cursing through
the sludge, leaving the Five-Nine's, and

BOOM! Thunderclap, then darkness.

There amid the giggles, I learned
that the end will be neither a bang
nor a whimper. It will be boys
hooting at girls squealing in the dark,
and a teacher's tired sigh
knowing he's lost them all.

Mason Jar, with Holes in the Lid

—for Eli

The body poisons the body—
Sjögrens, glaucoma, lupus—
because pain is all it knows.
Birth. Weaning. The violence

of eating: the tearing down
of life stolen from other
bodies to bolster up our own.
The dissolving of life into

calcium, proteins to build muscles
that pull triggers. To produce blood
that feeds tumors. Migraines
and torn ligaments hobble us.

To hold our souls bouncing inside
this glass cage like angry fireflies.

After Another School Shooting, I Cook Red Beans and Rice

I can't hear the TV news
over the soothing static
of diced onion in the pan.
States away, children bled.
In my kitchen, oregano
and cayenne bloom over celery.
Then broth, kidney beans soaked overnight.
Basmati. An hour later,
comfort. Food.

My bowl is warm, heavy, like my son
asleep on my chest. I can't stop
things, or start them. I can only
cook dinner, sit at table with wife
and child, and eat.

Ruah

If *wind* is also *spirit,*
then last night's gusts were

the ghosts of Trojan soldiers.
See the javelin pine-limb,

Paris's first shot without
Apollo's aid. The missile

missed Hector's slayer
and gouged itself instead

in the spongy flesh
of my rain-soaked yard.

May I Cut In?

You tap, shuffle on your momma's bladder
and the face she makes is strange—

somewhere between grimace and grin.

Still too small to be belly-felt,
your dance is a private one with her.

I'm a prom wallflower watching

the glam couple parade across the gym floor.
She wraps around you, eyes closed, and sways

to your twined rhythms. May I cut in? I want to feel

you press that sweet discomfort into my soft insides.
I want to hear the syncopation of my breathing

and your beating—a fluid groove I can't get in to.

Pulse (2)

Pregnant, again, then she bled, again,
around week nine, again.
No need to worry, we lied.

On the way to the doctor's,
quiet covered us like a poor kid's ill-
fitting charity coat. Waiting room:
admissions, paperwork, waiting, ugly
art in the lobby, small talk, forced
smiles and lunch plans, waiting.

The nurse's voice split the harsh
light as she invited us into the sonogram room—
dark, quiet, soothingly close.
And in that darkness,
your pulse.

Independence Day

This day, set aside to remember
the cry of mortar and musket
now silent. We fill the silence
with our own ordnance—
sparkle, starburst, shimmer:
a million micro-novas that dazzle
but soon die like unfortunate fireflies.
Freedom celebrated with amateur
pyrotechnics, assembled
overseas. All meaning unknown
to the mother who packs the powder,
the widow who tapes the label,
the orphaned child who fills
the boxes. With these fruits
of labor we bask in the light
of liberty.

Rachel's Curves

Natural, simple. Agile. Her right leg,
above where the knee was, gently caps
itself closed as the dome slides into her

prosthesis. A hug places her shoulder
squarely in the palm of my hand, like
a baseball. Expanded by her crutches,
her deltoid flexes gently, confidently,

with grace. Her left calf, supporting almost twice
its intended load, flares out—an unfurled
awning in the breeze—but calmly tapers
back in toward a delicate ankle.

A laugh slips through her smile and swoops
skyward. Its high, wide parabola opens
infinitely upward and hangs there.

Unborn, Daughter

I
Before

Before you smell like too much perfume
for boys I don't like, and before you
smell like your great grandpa's stale Pall Malls
and whiskey vapors, I'll be drunk off
of your slight warm sweetness,
like an uncut orange. Thank you.

II
Fertile

Her blood returned
too early, too heavy;

its temporary absence
denoting the presence

of one who lay
forming inside.

This body-to-be
ceased being

and returned to
the scattered state

from which it arose—
a flower regressing

from blossom, to bud,
to seed—and, like

seed, or ashes, spread
itself to be absorbed

into the moist soil.

III
Money For Nothing

We had to laugh when the bills started coming.
The anesthesiologist, the nurses, the hospital,
and the doctor's fee for the D&C itself.

It would have been cheaper to have the baby,
she chuckled through tears, both of us shocked
at how much this miscarriage cost us.

IV
Silent Night

The flame kissed the wick, and light was born
in front of the ultrasound printout of her unborn
who stopped growing in the ninth week.

She sat back and closed her eyes
against the candle's glow, the match-smoke
spiraling like dirty incense.

The bitterness has gone, mostly,
and in its place is this ritual, her own
little Advent. The breathing,
the light, the picture: all as quiet
as the candle's shimmering heat.

V
Pulse (1)

I could barely see the petite
heart pulsing inside of my wife.
A shimmer, a throb,
One hundred and fifty-two beats per minute,
the sonographer smiled. Perfect.

Three weeks later. She cramped, bled.
The ultrasound showed you, little runaway,
nowhere to be found. Silence shoved a stone
in our mouths, tasting of salt, bile.

As doctors removed what you left,
what was left of you, we
offered this oblation: a womb
too empty to be used as a metaphor.

If Basho Taught High School

*

A girl with Chanel
earrings asks me a question
about Emerson.

*

Test: the eraser
ends of their pencils dance like
little dervishes.

*

The autistic boy
finds God in the right angles
of the hall's lockers.

*

A martyred French fry:
foot-flattened and filthy on
the lunchroom floor.

*

Two P.E. kids play
catch. One, National Merit:
his friend, Down Syndrome.

*

The janitor hums
"Deck the Halls" as he pulls down
tinsel from the wall.

The Xerox Dukkha

This copier runs like an old man's prostate:
a couple of good shots, then it seizes.
And I'm sweating, cursing, trying
to get these poetry handouts run off
for my American Lit class.
But the copier won't let me—
it refuses to reproduce
Williams' old woman enjoying her plums;
her ripe juicy solace is a smear—
sucked out across the paper.
I clang and howl and rumble
and pull mangled sheets from
the machine's guts.

It pisses me off. It pisses
me off. It pisses me
off.

A colleague has placed
a wooden statuette of the
Laughing Buddha on the machine.
His well apportioned belly soothes
the ember of my anger, keeps
it from flying into and igniting the bin
of wrecked pages.

I crave these copies, thus I suffer;
my eightfold path blocked by
my three-sheet handout.

Dearest Gautama, may I lose myself
in the feeder, the collater, the toner drum.
May my middle path be as unsullied
as a newly opened ream of high-fiber bond.

Each Empty Desk

Chapter 3: Cloven

    (for Lanie)

I

I shortcut through the cemetery
and cursed last night's snow
for making me late for work.

My brakes shrieked as a doe and two fawns
dashed across the dirt road. Their tracks
took bites from the blind white earth.

II

A month later, at her grave—
brittle yellowed grass haloed
a bald patch of earth embossed by a hoof.
I hear her in this print's pressing;
rapid and alive.

Chapter 4: The Confession of B.G., student and thief

    (for Mason)

"I'm proud of my crimes: possession
on a school campus, and paraphernalia.

But there's more—truancy, breaking
and entering, petty larceny. I didn't
get busted for these, but I'm still proud.

I'm guilty of silence: of not telling
the cops that I broke in to steal
the coke, the pipes, whatever shit
I could grab, just so Mason's mom
wouldn't find it before the funeral—
just my luck that the dogs came sniffing
that day. I'm guilty of not kicking
my principal as he barked
at the cops to *cuff that trash
and get him out of my school,*
that his job would be easier if I'd
*just overdose like that loser
friend of yours.*

I'm guilty of letting him go,
not stopping his train wreck sooner,
not wringing his sorry neck.

The picture on my dashboard
is how I remember you, Mase:
not looking into the camera,
eyes beyond the frame
like you couldn't be held."

Trabajar te Pone en Libertad

In Morton, Mississippi, six-hundred-and-
eighty souls were arrested by Immigration
and Customs Enforcement to keep America
safe. To keep America safe, one-thousand-
three-hundred-and-sixty brown hands were
chrome-cuffed and cattle-led from the cramped factory
floor into cramped unmarked vans; hands that hours
before were still metal-clad in chainmail gloves to protect
the chicken thighs ripped from the machine-split carcasses.
The children of some of the six-hundred-and-eighty
workers stayed at school when the bell rang. Instead
of seeing their parents, they were greeted with pizza and
Pepsi and a safer America. To keep America safe, the
the plant lines stopped. The plucked corpses hung like ghosts.
The factory floors are kept cold, but untended chicken
is still unsafe. To keep America safe,
the poultry wasn't processed, wasn't moved
into the ice bath and frost packing. Bacteria
crossed skin's porous border, injected itself
into the meat, now rendered inedible and incinerated,
dusting the land with thin ashes, just
to keep America safe.

In the Absence of Meteor Showers

—for JB

Donald Hall outlived Jane Kenyon,
unlike your grandfather
who shot himself a few days after

giving you a copy of Hall's *Poetry
and Ambition*. When the poet
visited campus to lecture, you

stayed tucked in your dorm room.
In the auditorium, Hall likened his
early floods of inspiration

to a moonless sky spangled
with falling stars—sudden, fleeting,
unpredictable.

*But now, in the absence of those
meteor showers, I find myself
relying on form, like this,*

and read a poem—nine syllable lines,
nine lines to a stanza, nine stanzas—
about his friend Liam's suicide.

JB, here's what you missed: Hall's aged voice
floating like bonfire sparks that
mingled with stars before cooling

and falling beneath constellations
that, for all we know, stopped
burning centuries ago.

Body in the Freezer, for Love

When Bailey died,
we stuffed him in my freezer
since my friend Liz's fridge was too small

to hold her own dead dog.
Duct tape barely held the door shut against
the double-garbage-bagged beagle.

She couldn't afford to get him cremated,
so he stiffened next to my ice cube trays.
That night, we headed north

on US 51 and down a fire road
cut into the old-growth pines.
Greer read from the Book of Common Prayer;

John lit sage; I dug the hole; Liz wept;
and Bailey, who bolted onto Saint Mary Street
and didn't see the Volvo,

lay curled in the back of Liz's Jeep
as his plastic shroud pulled the humidity
from that soft April night.

Vigil

1.   Keep Watch

My back spreads like oil
on the nursery floor. His body
cradles the fever. When cries
wake me, I won't be confused—
ibuprofen dropper in hand—
and talk myself back to sleep.
Yes, I'll be sore come morning,
hoping to outlast what ails him.

2.   Scan

Swaddled in lead and wailing,
he quieted when the table
rocked him underneath
the CT's crosshairs.

Slides stacked on the screen,
showing infection packed
in his sinus cavities.

I hold him long after that night's lullaby.
The surgical litany replays itself: sinuplasty,
adenoidectomy, ear tubes. Nothing
to worry about, the doctor said.
We rock. I study
his hair, waves of thick blond
crashing over his fontanel.
I feel that tide—back and forth,
back and forth—still rocking
long after I set him in his crib.

3.   Red Scare

Upright on his
haunches, red running

from his mouth
like the clock's

LED's. Red like the blood
I'm sure this is,

complication from
the surgery his

one-year-old body
couldn't handle.

Red like the children's
Tylenol the doctor instructed

us to give before he warned about
post-op nausea,

a normal reaction
that isn't cause for panic.

Notes for the Funeral, Two Decades Beyond Her Prognosis

—for the Avalons

When I tell you about the memorial service,
here's what you shouldn't think about:
Keesha's brain tumor, the surgeries
and infected shunts, speech therapy,
more infections, the Special Ed classes,
oxygen tanks, pneumonia, the at-home nurses,
the twenty years doctors said she wouldn't live.
Forget Billy's teacher salary barely covering
the bills, Jana's back strained from lifting their daughter
into the car for all those trips to the hospital,
the last of which seemed so routine, Keesha's
blood oxygen still in the 90's,
and the sleep she fell into that morning—
Pentecost Sunday, that day of words and fire—
and her final breath, unlabored and solid.

Instead, I focus on their twined hands
in front of the white-shrouded casket.
Billy and Jana's whole bodies awash
in a gully of light from the church's windows
as the children's hymn fills the sanctuary,
her favorite one:
Little ones to Him belong.
They are weak, but He is strong.
Yes.

Mothers' Day Plans

—for Heather, after burying Rainer, aged two

Walk down to the riverbank. Kneel. Scoop
as much of the damp earth as you can. Fling it.
Listen to the wet thud. Keep
digging. When you hit clay, pull up a handful.
Stop for a second to watch the Mississippi
limp past. Ignore the loud barges and Beale Street.
Breathe the mildewy air. Feel its thickness spread.

That clay in your hands? Shape it now. A bird.
A tiger. A bunny. Anything. But know this:
there will be no miracle. When you set it down
next to the water, it will not spring awake and
dash away. Leave it.

Now go home. Do not wash yourself.
Make dinner. Chop parsley, toss it in vinegar,
use your hands. Taste, and note the river grit.
That clay beneath your fingernails will always be there.
The tiny statue you made won't dissolve back
into geology. It's still here. Unseen
but surrounded, hugged by that warm brown muck
of itself.

Recipe, for Caitlin

Shred your New Year's travel plans
when Heather's toddler dies.

Soak peas overnight.

Arrive in Memphis. Be surprised by the cold.
Hold her.

Dice one onion, one green bell pepper, two cloves
garlic. Sauté. Add salt and pepper (to taste)
and two tablespoons thyme.

Read a poem at the funeral. Tattoo it
onto your breath. Feel its weight
as it carves itself into you.

If you're off the vegetarian
wagon, add diced ham or
smoked sausage.

Learn about the Southern tradition of eating
blackeye peas on New Year's day as a
talisman for good luck. Have a bowl or two.

Add peas. Cover with broth. Bring to boil,
then simmer uncovered for an hour.
Watch the steam wisp and
tumble away.

Go home.

Months later, get a package from me in the mail
of dried blackeye peas, one pound. Because
you gave up your new year for a friend
and deserve to start over, again, for yourself,

because none of us know what the hell to do
after a two-year-old dies except go to the funeral
and read poems and feed each other.

> *Adjust seasonings. Garnish with hot sauce and*
> *sliced green onion, if desired. Serve over rice.*

School

An unkindness of ravens
A murder of crows

But what collective noun to describe
teenagers?

A rabble of butterflies
A murmuration of starlings

How to signify their singular motion? The
darting through the tides of adolescence?

A passel of possums
A rhumba of rattlesnakes

Scattering from predators, surrounding prey.
Fluid and rapid and unified and airless.

A gam of whales
A pod of dolphins

What word to capture this behavior, learned
and instinctive, flowing and ringing in their minds?

Punch Lines

The bruises on her face have faded
to an ugly mustard like old bookpaper.
My friend Jane offers this joke: You know what
all battered women have in common?

And after a perfect pause, she delivers the punch
line— They don't fucking listen!—striking
her hand with each stressed syllable
that mimics her ex's drunken rage.

She smiles, dotted with ointment and irony,
but I see her swollen eye wince at each pop
of her hand on the other, each sound
pulling at the upturned corners of her mouth.

Instructional

Figure 1:
Note the lifeguard's approach to the drowning victim. While the preferred method of approach is from the rear of the victim, the lifeguard here has chosen to swim towards the victim head on.

Figure 2:
Note the lifeguard's surprise at how quickly he and the victim ended up on the bottom of the pool.

Figure 2.1:
Having ignored his training thus far, the lifeguard now begins searching the depths (pardon the pun) of his memory. Note the look of concentration blended with absolute terror on the face of the lifeguard. Also, note the shafts of sunlight filtering through the freshly-chlorinated water and how the victim's grasp, if above water, would look more like an embrace of two dear friends.

Figure 3:
In this situation, the guard exhales in an attempt to make his rather ursine frame smaller. He also tucks his body into a ball in the hopes that the victim will not want to follow him further down. It's a risky move because

Figure 3.1:
This "suck-tuck-and-duck" technique works quite well on the water's surface. Exhaling is not recommended for individuals stranded on the bottom of the pool.

Also, normal victim psychology is a moot point in this situation, as the lifeguard is currently employed at a camp for adults with mental handicaps. The victim (weight: approx. 200 lbs. above water) has an I.Q. of 65 or thereabouts. While intelligence typically flies out of the window in near-death situations, do not ignore the victim's mental capacity as a reason for him ratcheting his grip on the guard as he exhales.

Figure 4:
Note the lifeguard regarding the bubbles dancing, almost drunkenly, towards the surface.

Figure 5:
Dead lifeguards can't save anyone. The guard remembers his instructor, a plain-spoken but well-regarded expert in the water rescue field. *If you think you're going to die, elbow the sonofabitch in the ribs.*

Figure 6:
Note the expanse now existing between the victim and the lifeguard. Also, note how an aforementioned sunshaft illuminates the water between them like a campy movie special effect.

Figure 7:
After getting some air, the guard has now returned below the surface. Note the look of confusion on the victim's face. You've done this, too: in a crowded room and you're conversing with someone; you turn to get a drink from the bar, and when you return

to the conversation, your companion has evaporated. So you hold your drink, maybe take a sip, and wonder what you said that was so ridiculous that would cause him/ her to pounce on the first chance at escape.

At any rate, note how the guard now approaches the victim from behind, wraps his arm in a cross-chest carry over the shoulder and across the rib cage, and pushes their way off the bottom of the pool.

Figure 8:
The rest is almost too boring to narrate: the sidestroke to the pool deck, the sputtering of water from the victim's lungs, the guard's co-workers roughly slapping him on the back. *Nice one, Baywatch!* or *I bet that was the longest three seconds of your life!* Note the lifeguard's smile. Whether he's posturing coolness or just happy to be breathing is unclear.

Caesarian Liturgy

—for Karen Cole, M.D.

I watched her scrub over the stainless
steel lavabo—under the fingernails,
up to her elbows: a medical mikveh.

As she washed, the only things that existed
were her hands. My wife, the operating room, me:
all rinsed away as she prepped to pull my son

from his watery nest.
Those unsoiled hands were his last
embrace of cleanliness before

being handed to me.

Each Empty Desk

Chapter 5: Curve

(for Callie)

Centrifugal force
pressed me against the car
door, like a spooning infant;
that lazy S turn in the interstate
by the city waterworks;
same turn that yanked
her through her windshield.

Chapter 6: Retouched

(for Sean)

The photographer lassoed his face
on the computer, sliced it
from his junior yearbook shot,
slid the image onto a body
about the right size.
A few clicks, some shading,
and his senior portrait was finished.
Extinguished light, now captured

His seat at graduation was swallowed
by the sea of his classmates; his place
in the annual remained his own. The photo
was fiction, replacing the hard fact the twisted
car, I see this easy grin, this lie I want to believe.

Circadian Arrhythmia

Cicadas jackhammer into the smooth asphalt
of the night's silence while sleep evades me.

Sandman. Hypnos. Somnus. All forsake me.
I would even welcome Anubis to embalm me

just a little. Change positions. Warm milk.
Read. Meditate. The clock's numbers

bore, thump, rattle like angry marbles in my brain.
Dawn. Not a simile for a new beginning; it's more like

a bully who sniffs out wimpy prey on the playground.
Bastard won't even knock me out. Alarm clock reminds me

of how it can't wake me up from a sleepless night.
Cold cereal. Shower, shit, don't trust myself to shave.

Outside. I am a dull razor scraping across the blank face
of my yard. An owl hoots. Ten A.M. He should be where

I couldn't go last night. He should be sated on mice
and dreaming of hunting tonight after the moon rises

and the cicadas throb like the tide.

Delta

In scientific symbolspeak
Delta (Δ) means change. But here
between Yazoo City and Memphis

Delta means changeless.
It's a pyramid built atop fertile
soybean and cotton fields.

The landscape itself needs no
variation, no hills or dips, just
flat acres of farms, roads, houses.

Here, hands that harvest
aren't the same ones that count profits,
just like it's always been.

The Boulder, the Plexiglas Window

—for Gitone

Driving to the prison to visit, I thought
of your name yanked from my roster,

your letters in my desk drawer. How you'd
skip gym to come read in my classroom,

how you'd given a friend a ride to work,
how the DA mutated that into Accessory

After the Fact. Visiting you on Easter Monday,
and how I would have trembled

and been amazed to find you not there
in an empty cell.

Jesse's House

The downtown pavilion serves him well,
rotting in the shadow of the Governor's Mansion,
shielding him from rain and sun under

its ugly green patina. His stained bedroll
gets tucked under brittle-dry shrubs
while Jesse perches on the curb,

hawking the bracelet he dug
from the gutter a few blocks back.
Gotta pay to get into that shelter, man.

I tell Jesse not to give me last week's line
as I hand him my weekly offering of two
peanut butter and jellies, a banana,

and a few bottles of water. He hassles me
for another sandwich (*I got this friend. . .*)
and I oblige, grinning through his lie. Springtime,

my church would meet in his park. Jesse
would leave some bug spray for us
next to the table we used as the altar:

the same rusted can week after week,
like a note from a timid schoolboy to his crush

$18.13, After Taxes

1.   Public school teachers in Mississippi are paid, on average, six-thousand dollars less than their counterparts in other Southeastern states.

2.   I have taught in Mississippi public schools for nineteen years.

3.   Governor Phillip Bryant (R—Mississippi) served two four-year terms.

4.   He signed eight state budgets that included teacher salaries.

5.   It is not uncommon for teachers to take on extra, part-time work.

6.   Once a week and the occasional weekend, I work at a local bookstore.

7.   This sometimes involves off-site signing events.

8.   Governor Phillip Bryant (R—Mississippi) has published an illustrated memoir of his eight years in the Governor's Mansion.

9.   The Mansion, a Greek Revival structure built in 1842, cost fifty-thousand dollars at the time.

10.   In 2019, that total would be one-million, three-hundred-forty-three-thousand, two-hundred-and-seven dollars.

11.   The book signing was held at the Governor's Mansion, which occupies a two-acre plot in downtown Jackson, Mississippi.

12.   When I arrived at the Mansion in my dented Honda Civic with four boxes of Governor Bryant's memoir, the scrolled columns beckoned me to bow prostrate to their own alabaster magnificence as the guards did a perfunctory search of my car under the shade of the centuries-old pin oaks.

13.   I unloaded the books myself.

14.   *The Mississippi Governor's Mansion*, authored by Phillip Bryant (R—Mississippi) costs thirty-two dollars and forty cents, with tax.

15.   I sold twenty-seven copies.

16.   Eight-hundred seventy-four dollars and eighty cents.

17.   Federal minimum wage is seven dollars and twenty-five cents an hour, before taxes.

18.   I worked two-and-a-half hours.

19.   The event was catered.

20.   I helped myself.

21.   The brie was warm and silken and spread across my tongue like an aggressive kiss from a drunken lover. It was accompanied by blackberries the size of my thumb, sugary and tart, almost pregnant with flavor. Even the seeds tasted good after I dislodged them from my teeth. The prosciutto, translucent thin, was a weeping violin solo in an empty cathedral.

22.   After the event, I packed the remaining books into my car.

23.   When I got home, I repaired a leaky shower faucet myself: seventeen dollars in supplies, about an hour in labor.

24.   Governor Phillip Bryant (R—Mississippi), having lived in government-supplied housing, hasn't paid for home repairs in almost a decade.

Exodus

I'm lonely as hell driving through Zion,
Mississippi, with the blues streaming
through my car. My grad school
buddy Steve, Jewish kid from Boston,
played a mean blues guitar:
Blind Brisket Rosenberg, I'd joke
as he riffed John Lee Hooker.
He'd kid me, a Southern Episcopalian,
about oppressing him as I warned
that the cafeteria's pork ribs weren't Kosher.

It makes sense that the downtrodden
sing each others' songs, that Zion
was founded by freed slaves,
its sole house of worship
a Missionary Baptist Church—Only Full Gospel!!
the marquee proclaims.

In my house, back door open to
let in the crickets' song;
no prophet Elijah comes to claim his seat.
I sip sweetened iced tea and scoop
hummus onto pita. No choir for my
little Eucharist, just Hooker on the stereo:
I'm drifting and drifting,
Just like a ship out on the sea.
Well I ain't got nobody
In this world to care for me.
I don't sing along—only hum
since I'm planted home.

Inheritance

It doesn't run through my family
like Dad's broad shoulders, Mom's habit
of humming to herself:

                the depression floods,

and I swim in the confluence
of low serotonin and suicides. Thus my pink pill
each morning before I look into my son's eyes,
brown-flecked and green, like mine.

A Reminder

I wanted to write a poem about swimming,
but R.E.M.'s "Nightswimming" keeps swirling
through my skull. Because Sexton was right—
the music remembers better than I do.

Summer camp, illicit late nights in the lake.
Innocent, recklessness in water. Our clothes
in sacred piles on the dock. No looking, no
touching, but aware of each other's skin.

Water cradled both the noon-sun's warmth
and our bodies, stripped except for moonlight.
Years later, late August, wife and son asleep.
The piano melody warms. The accidental glance,

fingertips on a shoulder. The liquid calm.
Emergence and redressing. September's
coming soon, then the strangled cold of November.
Pull, breathe, kick, glide through the quiet night.

The Neatness

Flowers: mostly roadside thistles
duct taped in a spiral on the street sign's post.

Pine sprig weighted with ornaments,
and his sign—*Homeless, hungry,*

Merry Christmas!!!!—sporting
a stained Santa hat.

There's no anarchy in poverty.
Only minimalism's precision,

the tinsel's choreography
in the steely December wind.

Medically Excused Absence

His mom e-mailed me, let me know
he'd be missing Friday's test. Surgery,

for the self-cut scars and pentagram
he branded on his shoulder. The plastic

surgeon calls it "scar revision," she said.
I English-teacher smiled at this. Revision.

A fresh look. A clean page.
I scrawled on a Post-It note: *G.B. surgery Friday*.

Ripped it off the block, gummed it to my computer monitor.
On the next sheet, my words left an impression—

a ghost note echoing what was taken away.

Composition

To paraphrase Faulkner, artists lie.
There is no magnolia tree. There is no mockingbird.
When we consume art, we bed ourselves with deceit.
Another way to put it: Shut up, Bob Ross.
Those scratches of phthalo blue don't look
like a waterfall, until they *do!* and you want
to dive in because there are no rocks beneath,
only a coolness so pure you could breathe it—
Your clothes abandoned beneath a cluster
of green, wide-leaved trees. You're swimming
with a lover. Well, a former lover,
one whose picture you still keep on the dash of your
Honda Civic. Except, it's not a her; it's
photo-sensitive paper and dye couplers and light
bouncing around your retina. And that mix tape
you made her isn't really music—Sonic Youth
aren't singing "Mote," and when Lee
doesn't belt out *I am airless, a vacuum child*
you feel so bound to that idea, that no-
thing, you find connection to that snapshot,
that song, that car, that painting, that magnolia,
that landscape, that mockingbird
that never existed.

Lost in Translation

I.

I never forgot the word for "foreigner": auslander

They can't be escaped. Even in my Munich
hotel room, I found the Bible from *Die Gideons*.
Perusing pages, the occasional flash of recognition,
and suddenly I wound my way through the cold
city and toward Gothic steeples across the square.
Gray stone, stained glass, mumbled prayers
from some locals. I knelt: *Mein Vater,*
du bist in Himmel, sehr gut ist deine Name
and stopped. I had outprayed my vocabulary.

II.

From Chartres, France, to Oxford, Mississippi

Medieval monks walked paths just like this one,
winding around themselves during daily prayer.

It's been reproduced in paving stones near the university's quad,
its only pilgrims now are squirrels dodging students
who hustle to nine-o'clock classes. A windblown beer can
skitters across.

III.

And the spirit moved across the water

My buddy, the only atheist in his AA meetings,
says he prays to the ocean. Sometimes
he'll drive the three-hour trip to the coast
just to watch the waves. I asked if he sees anything
other than water crashing on the shore. He said
No just as the wind whipped around us. Maple leaves
danced like fire. Then, silence.

Each Empty Desk

Chapter 7: Lesson Plan Change

(for Jes)

Handouts stacked next to the box
of Kleenex I didn't want to use,

nor did I want to get to Whitman until
we had exhausted Dickinson. But that morning,

I copied from *Song of Myself*. As his classmates
filed in, Charlie stared with narrow,

probing eyes; Larson looked at the floor.
I started. Voice crack. Dammit. Start over.

No array of terms can say how much
I am at peace about God and Death.

I asked leading questions—the kinds
he handled well. I told them they couldn't

blame themselves, that suicide
is complicated. They shouldn't ask *why*,

yet, that question buzzed me like a fly.

Chapter 8: More than Words

(for Parris)

Her obituary would have made her laugh.

"Parris Wallace. Died June 23, 2013.
Arrangements: Breeland Funeral Home."

That's it? she'd mock-diva. *No mention
of my stern demeanor? What about*

*my Nobel Prize, or the orphans I rescued
from the fireworks factory? Silly writers.*

What wouldn't I give to nudge her pen and paper,
to write her life beyond her epilepsy.

Coastline

—for Greer

Sitting over the beach,
the aftertaste of
thunderstorms still lingering
in our atmosphere;
silent, save the occasional
gull and the clumsy tumble
of the Gulf.

Along the horizon, oil rigs
provide artificial twilight—
cool, yellow, clustered nebulae
scatter about perception's
edge and continue their
lazy rape of the earth.

You trace the specter-white
tan line of my watch
and smile.

Eyes closed and sipping water
kissed with lime, I exhale a sigh
in perfect frequency of a wave
passing into rest.

Each Empty Desk

Afterward

New school year. Desks
arranged just so. I don't remember
unpacking your ghosts, but there you are
in the corner, giggling conspiracies.
How will you trick me this week?
Your eyes in someone else's face,
your laugh in hallway stampede.
When I issue textbooks, I'll see your names
in my handwriting. *Gotcha, Dickson,*
I'll hear you all chuckle as you creep
behind the shadows and prepare
to leap.

The Naming of Things

—for your second birthday

Horth, right now, means the rocking
horse that you tilt, tilt, tilt yourself on
while yelling *yee-haw!!* Later,

it will be *rocking horse,* and later still,
old toy my grandparents gave me.
After it spends time as *rocking horse*

I used to have, it'll become a nice story
at my funeral about me laughing
as you'd pet its velvet muzzle or try

to give it your pacifier. The oak
rockers will dissolve into time,
and the horse will become *nostalgia*

and the *innocence of boyhood*
and w*hen I was little, I had a horse
like that, too.* But first, you've got

to pull your tongue back, flatten
it behind closed teeth. Let the *ssss*
flow around that embouchure like

a creek rock's ripples. My impossible
desire: for you to grow, Clydesdale-strong,
smart and kind enough to eulogize me well;

yet to remain diaper clad, trotting on
the living room carpet, lisping wildly.

Notes on the Poems

"Kokopelli"—The kokopelli is a Hopi deity who presides over agriculture and harmless mischief.

"Three for Sylvia"—Each poem finds inspiration from poems by/about Sylvia Plath

"Hartsdale Drive, 2004" is based on Richard Wilbur's poem about Sylvia Plath, "Cottage Street, 1953." "Bite" is based on Plath's "Cut"

"After a Faculty Meeting, I Read Plath" borrows lines from "Lady Lazarus," "Daddy," "Contusion" and "Edge."

"A Reminder" borrows lines from Anne Sexton's "Music Swims Over Me" and R.E.M's song "Nightswimming."

About the Author

James Dickson teaches English and Creative Writing at Germantown High School, just outside of Jackson, MS. An MFA graduate from the Bennington Writing Seminars, he is the recipient of Mississippi Arts Commission fellowships, was named High School Literary Magazine Advisor of the Year by the Mississippi Scholastic Press Association, and was invited to speak at the National Educators Association 50th anniversary celebration "The Promise of Public Education." His poems, book reviews, and essays appear in The Common, Ruminate, Hospital Drive, The Louisiana Review, Spillway, Slant, Poetry Quarterly, McSweeney's, Sylvia, and other publications. He lives in Jackson with his wife, their son, and a small menagerie of animals.

www.ingramcontent.com/pod-product-compliance
Lightning Source LLC
Chambersburg PA
CBHW031149090426
42738CB00008B/1266